RETIREMENT THOUGHT LEADERS

A Modern Guide To Retiring In The New Economy

Edited By Mark Edward Gaffney,
Henry DeVries, And Don Sevrens

INDIE BOOKS
INTERNATIONAL

CONTENTS

Preface

In this modern economy, retirement planning can be a complex task.

Every retirement plan needs to be unique. When you meet with a financial advisor, what are the right questions to ask?

Remember when formulating those questions, the views and opinions in this book are those of the authors at the time of writing this book, and do not reflect the opinions of the editors Mark Edward Gaffney, Henry DeVries, or Don Sevrens.

This book is designed to be food for thought. Obviously neither the publisher, editor, nor the authors are engaged in rendering legal, tax, or other professional services through this book. The information is for retirement education purposes only. Naturally views differ amongst professionals, and these authors do not necessarily agree with each other and do not necessarily endorse the views of the other authors in the book.

If expert retirement assistance is required, the services of appropriate financial, accounting, and legal professionals should be sought. Of course the editors, authors and the publisher shall have neither liability nor responsibility to any person or entity with respect to any loss or damage caused directly or indirectly by the information in this publication.

Mark Edward Gaffney
Tampa, Florida
October 2019

1

The Firm With A Different Approach

By Billy Evans

Everything about the way I entered the investment management field and how I created my firm was different—from the very beginning.

I don't get bogged down in details; I want to spend all my time helping clients. The approach is not something you will find elsewhere, to my knowledge. It makes our firm distinctive—and successful.

I'm Billy Evans, head of Evans Financial Services based in Marion, Virginia. My firm consists of four friendly support staff and myself.

Consider what makes Evans Financial Services distinctive:

My background. I grew up on a cattle farm in southwestern Virginia and my family owned a wholesale beer and wine distributorship. (That made me quite popular in high school for about six weeks until the kids realized I could not show up at parties with ten cases of beer). I had been interested in finances and planning but suddenly I inherited the process and details of selling the family business and investing the proceeds. That evolved into a career path with an industry veteran becoming my mentor.

My timing. I opened in 2008 during the Great Recession. People were fearful, even panicking. The task at hand was to calm them down and to reduce the volatility decimating their portfolios.

My business model. I wanted to spend my time helping and educating clients and creating customized portfolios for them—portfolios based on their needs and risk tolerance, designed to meet their goals in good times and bad. I found a Registered Investment Advisor who shares my philosophies and takes the compliance specifics off my plate, leaving me more time to spend with my clients. I researched many portfolio managers, talked with them and narrowed down to about one dozen whom I liked. They used a tactical investment style I feel is important in portfolio management. I am constantly monitoring them, and their strategies, and I keep abreast of new managers who come along. It's amazing what one man can accomplish starting with a blank canvas and not being bound by any "we've always done it this way" constraints.

Baby boomers (those born between 1946 and 1965) are the bulk of our client base. They are at two stages: the ones pondering retirement and wondering if they can afford to, and the ones having made the decision and wanting a game plan.

Those who come in for preretirement interviews often walk out with something they did not expect. The interview is a good opportunity for us to create a plan for when they do retire. Some joke about being just one bad day away from choosing retirement, so most need several scenarios to choose from, and different routes to take if life changes.

We have found that after we have done the planning, we often can tell them that with their lifestyle they can retire next year. Yet, these people often end up working two, three, or four years longer than they planned. We have given them peace of mind. They can work because they want to, not because they have to. It takes the stress out of their situation.

Of course, some have not saved enough to retire. We tell them they may have to work a year or two longer than anticipated. Or, they may consider maximizing the income potential within their plan or making a change in their lifestyle and retirement spending.

Boomers who already have decided to retire go through a two-step fact-finding and interview process similar to the norm. We don't have an account minimum—I have a hard time saying no to someone in need—but the bulk of our clients have $400,000 to $600,000 in assets up to a couple of million.

The interview process and the emphasis on their goals and their risk tolerance are close to the norm. As for the products we choose and as for conforming to established formulas—well, there we go again being different.

You've probably heard that portfolios should be split between so much bonds, so much stocks, and adjust the proportion as you age. The standard thinking is that different asset classes, say bonds and stocks, may move in different directions or with varying intensity as the economic cycles change. We have concluded from our research, however, that in times of severe economic stress, say the twelve to fifteen months around the dot-com crash in 2001 and the Great Recession in 2008, bonds have not been the safe haven everyone expected. Bondholders suffered too.

As a matter of fact, bonds may not be our first choice among fixed-income products, but that is a separate conversation.

We educate clients that the conventional wisdom of holding certain assets through good times and bad may not be the best course for them. Baby boomers, you see, are going to be the first generation to live statistically twenty to thirty years in retirement. Some may actually spend more years in retirement than they worked.

Clients want to know if they will have enough money to last through retirement. A simple flash test that some advocate is to take a figure, say 80 percent of their current income, and see if a retirement portfolio can be created to match or exceed that level.

We get to that number in a different way. We ask clients about what they are spending their money on and their sources of income. We are trying to pin down how much money they need month to month. Does the plan meet their risk tolerance? Will they have the core cash they need and a way to get funds for emergencies? We don't want them to have to change their lifestyle just because of finances.

As I mentioned, boomers will be spending decades in retirement. By the time they quit working, many have paid off the house and their cars. But when you look at the prospect of living for another twenty-five or thirty years, you are going to be buying replacement cars, you are going to face home repair or remodeling bills. Not to mention travel expenses when you have the freedom to go where and when you want. Statistically, we know that people will spend a lot more money annually from sixty-five to seventy-five, the go-go years, than they will from seventy-five to eighty, the slow-go years.

By now, you know that I want to spend my time with clients, not tending to details and distractions. That is why I came up with the concept of using portfolio managers to handle client accounts according to strategies—usually rule-based strategies—that are flexible enough to adjust if markets take a sharp downturn.

Here's how the process works.

I favor eight to ten strategies of the hundreds available. Often the managers we use already have created a rule-based system. Sometimes there are algorithms involved in the system. The analogy I use is that we operate like a nurse or doctor in a hospital, checking the patient's vital signs constantly. So, we are simply checking the vitals of the securities we hold versus the whole market daily. Most days there is nothing to change. But we check anyway.

When interviewing a prospective manager, I look at how they performed in the past when the wheels fell off the bus. Typically, they did

not lose nearly as much money as the market.
And that's why our firm is using them now.

I do due diligence and basically stress test
the manager's performance style. Later,
if a new strategy comes along that I like,
we may embrace it to make the overall
portfolio stronger.

These managers handle the securities side
of the market. Which brings us to the fixed-
income side.

I like bond alternative vehicles where the
principal is protected, preferably ones without
fees. I do not consider a vehicle *safe* or *safer*
unless it is guaranteed. The guarantees I
want are from a third party. I want more than
just the backing of the bank or institution
issuing the product. Recall that in the Great
Recession one large institution went under
and others were forced into marriages with
healthier partners.

We believe that our policy takes away some
of the full-blown market risk. In addition, we
believe that the way we manage securities
takes away additional market risk.

What are some of the products we use? Certificates of deposit guaranteed by a third party. Some insurance products meet that standard.

We use two of the five types of annuities. We use a straight fixed annuity that works basically like a certificate of deposit, but the money and the interest are deferred from taxes and there is seldom a big fee or payment associated with that. We use market-linked certificates of deposit, and fixed index annuities, and we are constantly looking for the best opportunities for clients from high-rated companies. You can have those products and not pay a fee.

I feel like the industry as a whole has a bad taste in its mouth from anything that smells like an annuity. That's because of the variable annuities popular in the nineties and early 2000s. The high fees involved really benefitted the sellers of the products, not the clients.

You will notice that I did not fall into the trap of saying the fixed-income side should be a certain percentage of the overall portfolio. That varies with the client, depending upon their income needs and especially their risk tolerance.

There is a concept in the industry known as sequence of returns risk. Meaning that if you retire and put most of your money into stocks just before the market tanks—say 2008—you are in trouble and may spend years trying to claw your way back. If you put money in just before a bull run—say 2012—and especially if you diversify, you should do well.

I have included a chart of some mathematical trickery. If you suffer a decline in your portfolio, maybe a drop from $300,000 to $150,000, that is a loss of 50 percent. But to climb back from $150,000 to your original $300,000 is a gain of 100 percent.

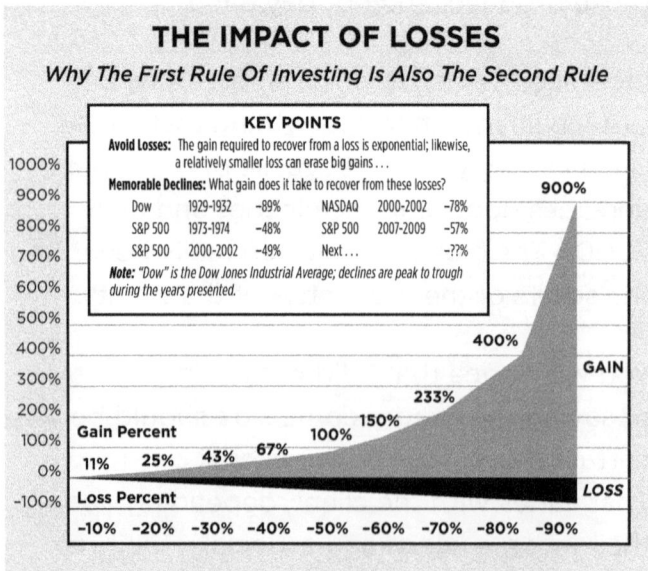

THE IMPACT OF LOSSES
Why The First Rule Of Investing Is Also The Second Rule

KEY POINTS

Avoid Losses: The gain required to recover from a loss is exponential; likewise, a relatively smaller loss can erase big gains . . .

Memorable Declines: What gain does it take to recover from these losses?

Dow	1929-1932	–89%	NASDAQ	2000-2002	–78%
S&P 500	1973-1974	–48%	S&P 500	2007-2009	–57%
S&P 500	2000-2002	–49%	Next . . .		–??%

Note: "Dow" is the Dow Jones Industrial Average; declines are peak to trough during the years presented.

Gain Percent values: 11%, 25%, 43%, 67%, 100%, 150%, 233%, 400%, 900%

Loss Percent axis: -10%, -20%, -30%, -40%, -50%, -60%, -70%, -80%, -90%

GAIN / LOSS

Trickery? Well, it is certainly counter-intuitive. The same amount of money but the drop is 50 percent while the gain required to climb back is 100 percent.

The best approach is to try to avoid that drop in the first place.

Recall that I opened my firm in 2008, hardly an auspicious time. I'm well acquainted with sequence of returns and the importance of avoiding that trap.

If I have done my job properly—perhaps leaving some chips on the table in the form of cash, perhaps investing in stages, perhaps recognizing that ominous times call for a greater amount of guaranteed fixed-income investments—the sequence of returns risk may be reduced.

Retirement planning is about more than money, it is about people.

In my highly nonscientific observations, people who say they are going to just lounge around the house in retirement tend not to live as long as those who have a passion, be it a hobby, volunteering, travel, or seeing the grandkids. It is not my role to be a life coach, but I do ask some diplomatic questions about their plans.

People come to retirement with widely varying levels of financial understanding. We spend quite a bit of time early on educating. We want them to know about mutual funds or exchange-traded funds (ETFs). We want them to grasp what we are recommending and why.

To that end, we hold educational seminars in addition to one-on-one sessions.

If they are struggling with the ins and outs of Medicare and Medi-gap coverage, we have a specialist to help them.

One of the things clients like about our approach, I've learned via referrals, is they typically never feel rushed. They don't feel pressure.

We try to hold the client's hand, so to speak, to help them, to educate them, and assist them in evaluating their market tolerance and making decisions for their financial future. This means that we sometimes need more than the typical two meetings to develop a plan or scenarios that they feel confident with moving forward.

About The Author

Billy Evans is founder and CEO of Evans Financial Services. He spends weekends with the family on the cattle farm he grew up on and helps his father with the hard-manual labor. Once a year, clients are invited to an appreciation event on the farm to experience a piece of Billy's life and be a part of the family.

2

Five Situations And How To Solve Them

By Bradley Johnson

Consider first these three scenarios:

Scenario #1. What grandparent would not like to leave money to their grandchildren in the most efficient way possible? Both from a dollar leveraging perspective, and from a control and taxation perspective, we can structure the transfer of a client's assets so that Uncle Sam gets a minimal amount of money, and we can plan for or even redirect unfavorable required minimum distributions (RMDs).

Scenario #2. I often see retirees with big hearts who make major or ongoing donations to their favorite charities. Once they know that in the large majority of cases, these donations stop at the donor's passing, they might want to meet to talk about planned charitable giving. Usually their heirs do not have equivalent charitable notions, but in some cases they can actually receive more money tax-free when the original donor sets up a plan to give away their most expensive (tax-wise) assets.

Scenario #3. A widow with a large two-story house is overwhelmed and thinking of selling it. Different voices are competing with different advice. She doesn't know all of the income or tax ramifications, or how to approach this decision in a logical manner. We can find order in the chaos.

I'm Bradley Johnson, a fiduciary Investment Advisor at Vimvest Advisors, and I love my work. I'm Florida raised and Florida educated. I received my undergraduate degree from the University of Florida and continued on at the Boston Institute of Finance. I've learned many powerful financial concepts, yet I would suggest the most wisdom I have accumulated is through learning to honor the Lord, love other people, and keep those priorities in line.

I bring this up because there is beauty to be found in understanding wealth management through the lens of faith.

Today it gives me great joy to be a part of the lives of so many retirees. I absolutely love getting the chance to teach them at a "Second Analysis" meeting how they might have a high percentage of their portfolio unnecessarily going to costs and fees. These costs, whether easy or difficult to identify, have often not been freely and transparently provided to them by their current advisors. If questions about hidden costs and fees have not been asked and remain unasked, it can be a huge drain to their portfolio.

Next at our meeting, I break down for clients the efficiency of their level of risk-taking. We can scientifically measure both the volatility in their portfolio and the historical returns of their given mix of asset classes or sectors they own in the market. Before our meetings, they typically have never had a way to measure the amount of risk in their portfolio. And of course they are quite pleased to learn that they can often reduce their fees, reduce their risk, and have an increased likelihood of increasing their returns.

So, let's tackle a few common situations for those in or about to be in retirement:

Giving To The Grandchildren

For our first situation, a useful tool that many clients may not be aware of is called "stepped-up basis." Stock that has risen dramatically over the years can be transferred at death, with the qualifying recipient able to use the current price as their cost basis. Suppose grandparents purchased the stock at $20 a share, but it is selling at $110 a share on the date of transfer. Their grandchildren can use $110 as their cost basis and only pay taxes on any further rise. The tax implications will be even less, which means we're maximizing the amount of money that they're receiving.

Charitable Donations

Making a major charitable donation and leaving money for your children does not have to be an either/or proposition.

A significant amount of my time is spent helping clients with assets of about $4 million to $10 million. They've worked hard, life has been good to them and now they want to give back to the causes they support.

It's rewarding to help make that happen. It's particularly satisfying to craft solutions that channel tax savings to the charity, and to use life insurance to guarantee, often more than the parents originally projected, their children's share.

These deals often involve collaborations with an attorney, a certified public accountant and myself. It's our job to be proactive for our clients instead of reactive. Different tools are set up and structured to get their whole financial house in order. Then the CPA and attorney can help us structure the private family foundation or charitable remainder trust so that we can use some of the income while realizing the least tax liability.

There are two different types of trusts we set up, each with different concepts.

With the charitable remainder trust, we donate some appreciated assets to a charity, get a present-day tax deduction, and allow the nonprofit to invest the assets in a manner which gives income to the donor. I had a gentleman in my office recently who donated $850,000 in 1992, invested aggressively in the markets of the nineties, and pulled off $70,000 a year in income for the last twenty-seven years. In exchange, the charity would keep the remainder upon the client's passing.

With the wealth remainder trust, it's a little different. The individual routinely controls and possesses all of the assets in their life, but upon passing, their most expensive assets (tax-wise) are donated to a nonprofit. Typically they have their heirs receive an equivalent amount in tax-free life insurance, with no strings attached to RMDs.

This solution works best for tax-sheltered dollars that have a ticking tax bomb, such as an IRA, 401(k), or a tax-deferred annuity. It satisfies the donor's philanthropic notions, and yet his or her children receive an equivalent amount with fewer strings attached. Charities themselves have increasing demands and limited resources, and studies show that in 91 percent of cases, contributions to charities cease upon a donor's passing. Typically, children or grandchildren may not have the same exact causes important to them. So, with proper planning, we can make sure that very substantial endowments can go to the charities while not taking away from the projected inheritance of the children.

To Sell The House?

A widow has just lost half of her husband's pension, 50 percent of her husband's Social Security check, and her marital tax deduction. She can no longer navigate the stairs in her massive two-story house, but she's afraid of what could happen if she tries to sell it. She doesn't know about the tax implications. She doesn't know if she can get a good price for the house. And if she sells it, what is she going to do with the money? Can she turn that money into enough income to be able to live with her friends at the senior community?

The people around her have differing concerns and are calling.

The children say, "Mom, the house is too big. You've got to sell it."

The doctor warns, "Your hips aren't up to that running around and climbing the stairs anymore."

The real estate broker says, "I have a buyer who wants to be in your neighborhood."

Each person has their own interests, none of which adequately satisfy all her concerns.

Seeking thorough guidance, she walked through our office door and we walked her through our "three-step review." We took a proactive look at where she is today tax-wise, where she is going to be if she sells the house, and what cost-saving strategies to implement so she pays the least amount in taxes.

She wants to be certain she gets checks in the mail for the rest of her life that are adjusted for inflation. If she sells her biggest asset, the house, our task is to create a reliable stream of income to meet her needs. We need to evaluate her risk exposure, particularly if her husband's inherited IRA turns down or if housing prices weaken.

We asked her what type of risks she takes with her money and how much of her nest egg she can afford to lose. Then we crafted a plan to protect the money that must be sheltered.

By going through this three-step process, we put her "financial house" in order before she sells her physical house.

The process works for any big financial decision. Whether you are selling a business, trying to get out of the stock market, or concerned about capital gains taxes, the three-step review ensures that the right questions are being asked before making any financial decision. It is a proven process that specifically identifies your needs.

Successful local real estate agents have come to understand the value of our three-step review, often reaching out to us to go through discovery with their seller before they actually sell the house. We clear up questions the seller may have and reduce hang-ups that could stall their deal.

For our widow in this scenario, we strive to ensure that she is making a sound, logical decision. While the house may have sentimental value for good reason, our discovery process helps us identify what we need the assets to do for us and points to a proper solution.

It's a difficult decision and often one of the first major decisions she is making without the help of her late husband. Why wouldn't you want a fiduciary in your corner, whose duty is to align their interests with yours?

The Happenstance Portfolio

Occasionally we have a prospective client walk in who has done a reasonable job of amassing savings with their work success; however, their investment advisors did not have an intentional, comprehensive process to help them along the way. One advisor suggested this, another that, and their portfolio may have grown, well, by happenstance.

Recently a woman walked in who was early on in her retirement. She had children, grandchildren, and had been a very successful nurse.

She had multiple other advisors in the past with different strategies and picked up various financial products along the way. None of them necessarily worked well together. They may have seemed good at the time when they were sold to her, but now she realizes that the pieces, like the discordant sounds of a symphony orchestra warming up, were not working in harmony.

We ran an analysis after understanding what she needed her money to do and made some discoveries. She had gone through multiple annuities. She had idle cash sitting in an IRA. She was losing money and not allowed to liquidate out of $100,000 in real estate investment trusts (REITs). Some items seemed to have just been dropped in there for no good reason.

Her portfolio brought to mind a bulging kitchen drawer with no organization. We started going through her assets one at a time. We looked through the annuities to see if they had certain caps, spreads, or participation rates. She quickly began to learn more about her investments than she ever had from her original advisors. In the last two years she had earned zero interest on her portfolio, even in the middle of a ten-year bull run. This was heartbreaking.

In her professional life as a successful nurse, she had been responsible for meticulously seeing that her patients' medications were given at the right time. She had to ask the right questions about patient allergies and do follow-ups to see that treatments were proceeding correctly. However, this same organized, skilled process was not occurring in her investment planning. Her financial life had gaping holes, the investment products did not work well together, and critical questions had not been asked by the initial advisors who sold them to her.

In a situation like this, we may spend extra time in the early stages of discovery. These problems arose because advisors were reactionary and quick to suggest products. We want to understand how the different components work, filter out the toxic investments and develop a strategy to unravel some of the mess. Our first creed for a client's financial life is to "do no harm."

Long-Term Care

As a fiduciary, I am not a proponent of most long-term care solutions. A prolonged illness can indeed be devastating to the family and their financial situation. Yet, most people don't have long-term care insurance because it is too expensive; it is an unregulated industry. Premiums can go higher and higher with decreased support until the individual is priced out. And all that money paid into premiums just disappears.

I *am* a proponent of "assets-based" long-term care, utilizing an insurance product where we can move a portion of the dollars to the sideline and receive a multiple on those dollars. We may be able to use that money to be leveraged and transfer it tax-free. The policy is written on an individual's life and can be accelerated to pay some bills before their passing.

It is a complicated matter but worth discussing with your investment advisor if you are so inclined.

Thank you for taking the time to read through these few retirement planning examples and how we have handled them. At Vimvest we welcome prospective clients to attend one of our seminars, explore our website or call for an appointment. We look forward to our annual or more frequent check-ups with existing clients and transforming them with a new-found confidence, encouraging them to make decisions based on logic and facts, instead of myths, misconceptions or missing pieces of information.

About The Author

Bradley Johnson is a financial advisor with Vimvest Advisors.

3

Retirement Planning With Some Special Touches

By Bryan Foster and Carol Carroll

We're different.

Some in the industry call us weird.

Yes, like the ugly duckling was weird in the beginning.

What we are is a son/mother firm. One that shows how to close the income gap in retirement, sometimes with a unique three buckets of income approach. We help clients traverse the Medicare supplement jungle and choose the policy that is best for them. (Yes, in this jungle cheapest is best and we can find that at lightning speed.) We go to meet clients on their turf—home, office or out amid the crops. We tell countless baby boomers they need to put themselves and their needs ahead of the kids and grandkids. (We show them an easy way to take the legacy issue off their shoulders. And we push them to go out and start having fun in retirement.)

Mom, with the alliterative name, has been in the business for thirty years and ventured on her own in 1998. She's the senior vice president now. Son Bryan, CEO, graduated from the Ohio State University—yes, he's a great football fan—and was on his way toward a career as a cardiologist. It wasn't the right fit, however, and in his heart he knew that the financial business had always been in his blood.

They may seem like two dramatically different fields but both help people with their quality of life, Bryan says. The transition was easy. It's helping someone with everything they ever worked for and everything they ever saved for their entire financial life.

BFFinancial is an independent firm, backed with the database resources of TD Ameritrade and some technology of its own.

We have the tools and the algorithms and the programs and all the new technology. Mom is old school leaning hard on the human factor; son is very much technology. We find that when there is a blend of the two, that really is the secret sauce. That's what makes clients happy.

Here are our approaches to some retirement aspects that make us stand out.

Closing The Income Gap In Retirement

Setting up an income for life and what they get depends upon the product you are writing for them. You know the size of the gap you have to close. So typically the solution is going to be an indexed annuity. We're going to look at one that doesn't have any fees. We're going to look at one that has a nice big bonus to increase the income base so that way they're getting extra money in their account, and there's even one right now that we particularly like, which continues making money even after they start drawing income.

The golden handshake, the armload of documents, and how we help you deal with Medicare. When people walk out the company door for the last time, the HR Department loads them up with a ton of documents. They need to get on board with Medicare (Parts A and B in the jargon) and select private insurance companies to cover what Medicare does not (Parts C and D). There is some urgency. If you put off signing up for Medicare, hoping you can avoid paying premiums for a while, think again. If you have turned sixty-five and are not covered by an employer's health policy, well, you'll be sorry.

We'll help fill out the forms. There is an open window in the fall when you can switch carriers. If you feel your carrier has raised premiums by an excessive amount, more than age related, we'll run a new comparison for you. The coverages for each company are the same; what you want is a reliable carrier that charges you the least.

This is a popular service and we find that many clients take us up on it.

It runs in the family, on our side of the table and the clients' side as well.

Ours is a family firm. But look across the table. We tend to work with families a lot.

We represented four generations—great-grandparent, grandparents, parents and son—until recently when the great-grandparent passed away. Their coverage varies by their life stage, of course, but just about every vehicle was represented. Annuities, estate planning, brokerage, life insurance.

We think the reason is that people trust us. This is what we do. This is where they are, and here is what they want to accomplish. What they want to accomplish is the most important thing.

Our slogan is: "Creating legacies, one family at a time."

Farmers can't take the time to see us, so we go for ride-alongs. We offer a complimentary concierge service. What that means is we'll come out to their office, their home. We have a beautiful, spacious office in town. But they are more comfortable in their own setting. Nine times out of ten, they will take us up on it.

We're in Ohio farm country and farmers don't have the time to stop working. That makes for some interesting visits. Farmers with modern tractors, they have air conditioning, stereo, GPS—the tractor basically drives itself.

We jump in, chat, pass documents back and forth. Farmers with ancient tractors, well, not so much.

The three-bucket system, not to catch rain, but income for you. We sometimes use a three-bucket system to finance retirement which we believe is unique to us. Sort of a play on the old-fashioned grocery money in one envelope, rent money in another. The first bucket is for five years, the second for the next five years. When the first is empty, we turn to the second. The third bucket simply repeats the cycle. By the time we reach the third bucket, it has had ten years to grow.

The buckets are split one-quarter, one-quarter, one-half. The first uses an annuity with a 3 percent yield. The second bucket uses a different kind of annuity with a 4 percent yield. The third bucket uses equities with a growth target of 6 percent a year.

The concept is that the third bucket replenishes the other two when they are used up.

"I can live off 80 percent or 90 percent of my preretirement income, right?" Based on our experience, that might work for the first couple of years. Those first two years are

really stressful and they are trying to penny pinch everything. Then they realize that retirement can be fun if they spend. Plus life tends to throw in surprises. It's like a budget that looks fine on paper but try living with it.

Boomers, you need to put yourselves first. We'll show you how to solve the legacy worry, but repeat after us: "Retirement is a time for fun. Retirement is . . ."

If someone is struggling in retirement, do we ever have to give them the lecture, you have to take care of your needs first and not become a burden on your children?

Yes, all the time. Baby boomers may be living like paupers even though they have plenty of assets, hundreds of thousands or millions of dollars because they want to leave it all to their kids. They pay bills for their kids, a new truck for the grandkids. Meantime they may be limiting themselves to really just one meal a day.

You have to tell them that they must realize their own self-worth and their own quality of life are just as important as anyone else's. Even those they love. We want to take care of and protect our family, but we don't have to be in lopsided equations here.

There's a way to do that financially, to enjoy spending your money while still leaving a guaranteed amount of money, the amount that you specify, to your kids. That beauty is called life insurance. So you just tell us what the number is and we'll run the examples and the illustration. The vehicle is guaranteed universal life.

But once we get your children's money set up, you must promise us that you are going to take care of yourself. You're going to go out and have some fun. Sure, you can pay to have the roof fixed, but then you're going to do the things you want to do.

The universal life policy is more costly than for a twenty- or forty-year-old but we're still leveraging the money. If you put $100,000 in, we want to see it pay out a minimum of $200,000 and $300,000 makes us happier.

So basically the legacy is in place for the kids. The parents are much more apt to stand up for themselves. "Yes, I'm going to go play." It is wonderful to see that transformation, the relief, to hear the sigh, to see the shoulders go down. "It's done. I did it. OK."

Downsizing, a way to stay young at heart, young in spirit, young in body. People may downsize immediately at retirement, perhaps buying a smaller house in a different state. They may move into an active seniors complex after the passing of a spouse. Shifting to assisted care is like renting an apartment. Only with them doing the cooking and you get three square meals a day. With activity centers, places to hang out. Everything on site from banking, massages, haircutting. Gyms with personal trainers. Excursions to entertainment.

In time skilled nursing or lockdowns (for Alzheimer's or dementia) can be arranged with adjustments in rent.

It is not cheap, Carol points out. One in Dublin, Ohio asks $500,000 up front for a couple with $50,000 a year in rent for five years. Life insurance policies eliminate financial risk from premature passing. It is definitely a premium service. They are getting what they pay for.

I have visited clients three or six months after moving in. They have shifted from sitting on the couch to doing betterment, to enjoying life again. Their demeanor changes. They are standing a little taller. Their skin is a little brighter. Their outlook on life has changed dramatically.

Once they have made the decision, we help with adjusting their financial plan. I have been doing this a long time. Not once have we been unable to find a match with a facility they can afford.

Our introductory, fact-finding process is quite similar to the norm in the industry but crucial to finding the best end result. The most important aspect is looking at what the client is trying to accomplish. Then we shop that information around. Like for an insurance policy, you take all their information and you shop it among all the companies. So who wants to give the most coverage and charge them the least and kind of summarize that. It is a three-step process: Where are you now, where do you want to be and how can we get there? One, two, three.

There are two main things we must do right. First, we must spend the time to understand the client's needs and wants and their risk tolerance. Second, we must select the right products and sufficient strategies to match them. For every plan we come up with, we check on their medical coverage. We want to make sure the entire plan does not collapse because of some medical issue.

We put on seminars, rotating among three retirement topics. But no seminar ever runs more than an hour. We see the clients' eyes glaze over. We think we hear the bell ringing now.

One last thought: We measure our success in the level of our client's happiness. And we're very good at it. This is why they pass us along to other family members, to friends. We do the referral business that we do because we do what we say and we say what we'll do.

About The Authors

Bryan Foster is chief executive officer of BFFinancial in Dublin, Ohio. Carol Carroll is senior vice president. More commonly, they are known as son and mother. BFFinancial Advisors of Dublin, Ohio, should not to be confused with a firm of the same name in another state. Look for them at www.bffinancialadvisors.com or pick up the phone and call 614-789-1644.

4

Bringing High Technology To Retirement Planning

By Margaret Hixon

Little did I know the career counseling I received thirty years ago would turn out so well.

I was a young woman from Tennessee entering the investment world and was paired with a top producer—an independent— associated with a national insurance company. "Margaret," she said, "Go independent as quickly as you can. You will be able to do a better job for your clients."

It took a little longer than anticipated but with the encouragement of my new husband Loren, I took this big step and opened my own company. That was before the Internet took off, before lightning-fast computerization was readily available, and before we could choose from a broad array of investment products we have today.

Now, Vimvest Advisors is an independent, full-service house with thirty employees and many millions more of assets under management. We have a spacious office in Sarasota, Florida and an executive center in St. Petersburg, Florida.

Vimvest has its own proprietary app, launched in February 2019, that enables clients to invest, save and give. Gone are the days of the traders yelling across a floor to match stock buyer and seller. Gone are the days of ticker tape machines and reams of paper used daily. Everything is electronic now.

Today, potential clients who are intrigued by my general seminars called "The Myths and Misconceptions of Investing," come into our office for a Discovery Interview. It is focused on gathering information and seeing if we have a good fit. They learn about tools that didn't exist in the olden days—software and apps that do everything from A to Z. We can "x-ray" a client's portfolio and do fee comparisons, including those sneaky hidden fees. If they ask: "Do I have enough to retire?" we can answer that, all with the push of a few buttons.

In February, Vimvest was proud to be one of just a few independents plunging into the 21st Century with an incredible technological advance. Some two years and $15 million after we started, we launched our financial technology (fintech) app that can instantly search thousands of products in a database for the ones with the lowest fees and best past performance. Ask a question and we'll search for you, or our clients can access our platform and do it themselves via phone or laptop.

Computers can do so much, yet they don't replace experienced, trained advisors. We're proud of ours.

With the growth of Vimvest, administrative duties now occupy much of my time, although I am still active on the fixed index annuity side. There are still many minefields in the investment world, however. Here I will touch on how to avoid products that are inappropriate for you and how to fix bad financial planning that fattens someone else's wallet instead of yours.

Retirement planning is about helping people and I see to it that we haven't lost the human touch. Prospective clients sitting in our conference room are surprised when Coal walks in and drops a toy on the floor.

Coal—yes, he's jet black—is our office greeter. He's an eight-year-old Havanese, a breed of dog from Cuba, who is perhaps ten pounds soaking wet. "Want to play?" he asks. Who can help but smile and momentarily forget the day's worry?

"Vimvest" is a coined word, a play on vim and vigor and wrapping oneself in fine vestments. It's easy for clients and staffers to get wrapped up in Coal.

Our typical client is aged fifty or older; most are baby boomers. Some 98 percent of our clients are ready to retire.

We have always offered safe products for income planning. We focus on income planning first to make sure it is achieved, and that people will not outlive their assets. Then we focus on growth after we feel we've protected the most important part of their investment. We have a strategy and the coaches to communicate it well.

With regard to insurance products, the arrival of the fixed index annuity has transformed the industry. It really revolutionized fixed products for investors who are conservative and looking for a 5 percent to 6 percent yield. These are tied ("fixed") to an index. They can guarantee no loss on your principal and have riders that provide some inflation protection. These vehicles protect your savings while allowing you to participate in some of the growth in a rising market.

Let's not confuse today's "fixed index annuities" with the "variable annuities" of a generation ago.

Variable annuities were very popular in the nineties. They are essentially a basket of mutual funds with lots of fees. Clients really do not do well with them because they are up against fees of 3 percent to 5 percent every year.

On the other hand, modern fixed index annuities just take an average. So, you get to participate and capture maybe half of the gain the market does, but you're not exposed to the downside in a market correction. You don't lose any of your principal due to fees; there is no fee structure.

I think of today's fixed index annuity as a bond replacement. Doing an asset allocation using a fixed index annuity replaces the bond piece so you don't have interest rate risk or suffer the volatility of the interest market. I consider fixed index annuities to have zero risk.

How do clients get to know us?

Whether they are looking to have a customized plan crafted for them or are dissatisfied with their existing program, most clients find us via our seminars or are referred by friends.

We call our initial conference a Discovery Meeting. We take their information and prepare reports for the next session. Our reports provide a picture of their financial health. Our software really pulls out information including hidden fees that may have escaped them. We go over all of this during the second session. We expose overlapping fees and under-performance in a report that lays it out in simple, easy-to-understand terms.

Most people have all of their assets in one area instead of having them diversified. We go over their income strategy and show them what may disappear and what may not if a spouse passes. Sometimes, there is a need for a third session to make sure they truly understand everything. It is vitally important that we spell out the difference between what they are currently doing versus what we can do for them.

Our reports are a proprietary piece of software available to us through Morningstar. This software turns out the data in a pretty format that laymen can understand. This access to data resources puts smaller independents on an equal footing with the mega-brokers while not being handicapped by the bureaucracy of a large institution.

"Do I have enough to retire?" is a question foremost in prospective clients' minds when they walk into our office. For that we turn to software called a SIPS Report (Structured Income Planning System). If we have determined what the income need is, we can put in all of the products tentatively selected and the software will tell us how well the product choices meet that need.

"How much can I draw?" is another main question clients have, and we can answer it through the advantages of the annuity vehicle itself and the software. The software has literally every annuity in the universe. When we're looking for an income and need to close an income gap, we can select a product inside the software and see which one is the best choice for the client based on the type of income they are looking for and their age. Then, we show the difference in the portfolio. It literally charts with built-in inflation factors. It shows pretty closely what they are going to be looking at over their lifetime.

I do have some pet peeves about greed-driven industry practices that put customers in inappropriate products, about the risks involved with Real Estate Investment Trusts (REITs), and about the continued use of old-fashioned variable annuities where high fees decimate the suggested rate of return.

We often run into products other firms have sold our clients. If the clients really knew what they were getting into with these products, they would not have picked them. Care must be taken in putting together a product for the client instead of just focusing on a commission. Our industry is no doubt challenged by a lot of greed.

REITs turn out to be quite risky. The trusts own a variety of buildings and pay out most of their income in dividends, tasked as ordinary income to the investor. With the exception of a few trusts traded on a stock exchange, the shares can only be sold back to the company. That may be a stand-in-line process and at 50 percent off, to boot. If the trust does not do well and has vacant buildings, for example, the investors who bought them will find out they lost half the value and half the dividend. So, those are really tough situations where people get tied up and can't easily remove their money. To prevent a run-on-the-bank type of situation, the trust can slow down the pace of withdrawals. It can take a quarter to a year or more to pull out money—your money.

In my seminars I talk about variable annuities and the misconceptions investors may have had about what they purchased, only to be crushed by the high fees involved.

Anecdotes make the concepts easier to understand. A doctor, newly arrived at age forty-nine, and his wife came to one of my seminars. I always talk about the "risk" side of things, the "safe money" side and what types of products are in each category. When I brought up variable annuities and REITs, they both looked at each other and said, "Oh my, I think we may have those." I have come to recognize that look and the kick under the table.

They came in to see me the next day. The doctor, a specialist, was very successful but burned-out, and chose to retire. They had chosen to live very conservatively and had built their wealth. I asked what they needed to support their lifestyle and he answered, "about $250,000." He also mentioned that the mega-broker had told him he would have to go back to work to close the income gap.

A few questions later I determined the doctor and his wife were worth over $10 million. What was the disconnect?

The brokerage had put all of the doctor's after-tax savings into variable annuities, some $6 million in worth. He had reached the limit in his IRA tax-sheltered account.

I called the mega-brokerage and discovered two horrible things the couple did not know. First, they were paying the insurance company $250,000 a year in fees. So, we found their income. The market had just had a ten-year bull run, but they were paying 4 percent a year to the insurance company and only cleared 2 percent a year, on average, on $6 million of their money. He should have doubled his money over those ten years. Second, these annuities did not have joint payout for husband and wife; only single payout. That meant, if he passed, his wife would be disinherited from the payout.

She started crying at the table.

It took a lot of maneuvering but eventually we were able to find another insurance company to take over these contracts. We were able to straighten out their portfolio and get them into a proper situation. They chose not to sue the firm because they did not want to go through arbitration.

Another couple who came in had 90 percent of their money in real estate investment trusts, and had already lost about half of their stake. I really do not believe in REITs. Only 17 percent of them meet their target returns. When you are income planning, you don't want to jeopardize somebody's income. We reduced the couple's holding as quickly as we could.

There are a number of common myths and misconceptions about retirement. At Vimvest, we're happy to clear up the confusion.

Epilogue

My passion for helping clients is a legacy of my upbringing.

I come from two generations of doctors. My grandfather was a surgeon who was called "The Button Hole Doctor." He developed a way to remove an appendix with just a one-inch incision.

My father was a radiologist and head of the department in Kingsport, Tennessee for more than twenty years.

However, both generations were broke when they died.

Today we can apply high-tech science to our strategies and generate income for life, something my family did not have in place.

Never, never, never jeopardize your lifestyle income.

About The Author

Margaret Hixon is president of Vimvest Advisors. She founded the independent firm thirty years ago.

5

A Firm Built On Children Telling Parents

By Micah Keel

Many people move to Florida to retire, to slow down and enjoy the good life. Our company is expanding rapidly in Florida with our first location in Sarasota. We are opening in Florida to continue our passion to help clients breathe easier about life and fuel our passion to help clients enjoy the lifestyle they have dreamed of when work becomes optional.

We are oXYGen Financial, the name that began on a play of words within the X and Y generations and helping them achieve their financial dreams and goals. What we learned about the younger generations is that somewhere between the ages of forty and fifty, most parents realize they have children who know more than they do and begin to ask them for advice ranging from technology solutions to how to handle their investments. We learned that many of our Generation X clients were getting deeply involved in their parents' finances and asked us if we could help their parents with retirement, taxes, long-term care and estate planning. It has been the children really driving the engine because they don't want to see their parents run out of money. That is how we morphed into a company that serves all generations, with retirees being one of our fastest-growing segments. Now, we can help all generations breathe easier about financial planning and can offer help to families across America.

At oXYGen Financial, we've created a completely new approach to financial planning through a high-tech and high-touch process. Most notably, we've created something called the G-P-S process, which is a proprietary system that is far more powerful than traditional asset allocation or traditional income planning. The G-P-S system helps us determine how much money each individual client should have in *growth* investments, *paycheck* investments, and *security* investments to maximize their situation while also overlaying a tax management plan to minimize taxes to the government. We have an extensive team of investment professionals who use our proprietary algorithms within the G-P-S system to maximize the way you should handle your assets.

As technology changes the way we do business, we are out of the box thinkers in the way we help retirees grow their assets and create more retirement income. We have created our own Warren Buffett and Jimmy Buffett portfolios to drive more income in retirement. Warren Buffett has always said his favorite holding period is forever, so we are extremely selective in the way we build fixed income and choose equities that we plan to hold for the long term. We consider interest rates, taxes, the economy and geopolitical conditions. We also have the Jimmy Buffett component. Jimmy has a famous song that says it's always 5 o'clock somewhere. With all of the information coming through media, social media, and the internet, we need to be alert to see where opportunities are and be strategic about making those moves to capitalize on where it is 5 o'clock. By using this combination, we can truly help our clients protect their wealth and maximize their current retirement income.

It's extremely hard to know how to choose an advisor today, but we run under some very basic principles:

1. We act as a Fiduciary—I am bound by oath to do what is in your best interest as your investment advisor

2. We don't sell products—we don't represent any product companies

3. We have experience—our firm has more than three hundred years of experience and more than twenty advanced designations including more than twelve Certified Financial Planners

4. We manage a lot of money—more than $1.4 billion

5. We have a high-tech and high-touch experience to suit the needs of every client

6. We are a boutique shop so you won't get lost as a name and number

We look at retirement as if you're running a business and a business has to make sound financial investments so that it stays solvent. We approach retirement the same way. We put you as the CEO of your family's retirement and then you hire us to be your CFO to make sure that your budgets are in line—to make sure that you're keeping up with inflation while also overlaying a tax management plan to minimize taxes to the government. Our plans include review of clients' insurance, wills and trusts.

We have the customary two or more meetings to gather information. During those meetings, we educate clients on running "their business," understanding the various tools that can help them to reach their goals. We also teach our clients ways to create passive income streams doing what they love to do.

In some cases, we have helped families take passion projects and turn them into income-producing businesses using social media. Why not turn your creative hobby into income? Etsy is a platform that helps artists and crafts people sell their handmade goods. Airbnb has absolutely exploded in popularity. Listing a room on Airbnb in your existing home—either on a permanent or short-term basis—is an ideal passive income stream because it uses an existing resource to generate money. We have helped some of our snowbird clients turn their second homes into vacation rentals that can generate income during the months they are not using the homes. JustPark is a platform that lets you rent out parking places. This is an ideal opportunity if you live near a popular venue. Do you have an RV sitting in your driveway? Rent it out! RVShare makes it easy for you to make money from a potentially under-used asset. We try to think outside the box when it comes to Passive Income Streams in retirement.

Of course, some clients may not be financially savvy, or have that entrepreneurial drive, perhaps recently losing their spouse who handled the money affairs. There is a lot to grasp in these sit-down meetings, so we add sessions at their pace. For a widow or widower, especially, we to try to get the children involved in the process. We want to make sure they understand what Mom or Dad is doing with their retirement savings.

We think *budget* need not be a dirty word.
Sure, some people despair at ever creating
a budget on paper that anticipates their
spending and what they can actually live on.
Our Certified Financial Planners put on what we
call our budgetologist hats and we put together
what their expenses are. First, we look at their
essential expenses, the basics. Then we look at
their lifestyle expenses, the niceties.

After we've calculated those numbers, we
show them what type of portfolio—how much
they need to have—to meet those cash flow
goals. We want to have their essential income
needs covered by secure investments, which
would be pension and Social Security income
streams that are dependable. Maybe there
is a rental property or home-based business
in the mix as well. The more diversified the
income sources, the better in our opinion.

If the client wants to use us, then we create
what we call a client dashboard. This is where
we input all of their investments, cash flow
and expenses. This is the clients' retirement
balance sheet.

What is a dashboard? It's a web-based
retirement plan that they can log into from

anywhere in the world, where they can collaborate with their kids, their attorneys, their CPA. It is interactive. It notifies them when their allocation gets out of whack. It notifies them when any updates have been made to the portfolios, updates from their investment advisor or just from the market.

Understanding cash flow is a very important part of retirement planning. If you don't have cash flow you can't really do the things you want to do in retirement. So we specialize in keeping the creation of a budget really simple. We also incorporate that into the dashboard so clients can see their real-life budget based on their spending. Once again, red flags can go up if they are getting out of whack. That's a process we manage and assess with technology playing a significant role. There are twenty-one different budget categories. It's a process that tells clients where their money is going. And in that process we identify which of the expenses are essential and which are lifestyle.

The dashboard has everything in one place. It helps because it's real. It's not just this thing you look at once a year. It's something that every time you log in it is right in your face.

But then that's how a business operates. You have to run your retirement as you would a business.

This electronic budget process does the work with a minimum of effort by the client.

Protecting your nest egg is often the missing piece of many retirement plans.

As we stated earlier, we think that managing cash flow in retirement is a key component to a successful retirement plan.

The reality is you can have the best retirement investment plan and the best budget in place, but if you don't address the fact that one or both spouses may need long-term care at some point in retirement you are really leaving your nest egg exposed.

So let's address a not-so-fun topic: long-term care expenses.

Long-term care can be a tough decision. After all, no one wants to think about themselves or their loved ones being incapable of living on their own. But every solid retirement plan should also address protecting your nest egg, so that means long-term care insurance or an affordable alternative is a must.

Take Bill and Peggy, for example. They were always good about saving for retirement; they worked hard and built a nest egg of $550,000.

When Bill was sixty-eight, he developed Alzheimer's disease. It wasn't too bad at first. Peggy used some of their nest egg to hire a home-care specialist to help with Bill a few hours every day. But as his condition worsened, Bill had to go into a nursing home.

Sadly, after five years in the home, Bill passed away. Peggy, now seventy-two, is healthy as can be for her age, but she has to work full time because her husband's stay in the nursing home depleted most of their savings.

Their story is not unique by any stretch; it happens to many retirees every year. However, with long-term care insurance in place, you can keep it from happening to you. At oXYGen Financial our independent insurance division will shop several different long-term care companies and get you quotes. Planning ahead can save you thousands of dollars and tons of stress should one of you need long-term care in retirement.

For those who have the means or what we call lazy money just sitting in savings accounts earning very little—say they are sixty or sixty-two and healthy—we like to utilize a three-pronged approach with a life insurance policy with chronic illness or long-term care riders attached. The policy provides long-term care in the event they do need it, but also it provides a death benefit if they don't have to use it. The life insurance passes to their family tax-free. Some policies include return of premium riders. What this means is if they ever find themselves in a liquidity need, the money they put into these plans can be returned to them. They don't get any interest on that money, but at least they get their principal back. That's the approach we try to take because a standard long-term care policy is so expensive and there's a possibility that they may not need it. This type of plan seems to make sense to our clients' children.

It's been a pleasure sharing our approach to retirement with you. We view retirement as just the beginning a new chapter. Our passion is to help clients breathe easier about life and this fuels our passion to help clients enjoy the lifestyle they have dreamed of when work becomes optional.

About The Author

Micah Keel is an author, market analyst, and independent financial advisor with twenty years of experience. He is the managing director of oXYGen Financial in Sarasota, Florida. oXYGen Financial is built on the principle of having a cost affordable modern-day family office. We are built to be the CFO of your family finances. Whether this is helping you with your retirement income, selecting cut-the-cord options, mitigating income taxes or thinking about a will or a trust, we can help you breathe easier about life. Micah was honored with the Five Star Wealth Manager Award in 2014, 2015, 2016, 2017, 2018, 2019. For more information on the Five Star Wealth Manager and the research/selection go to www.fivestarprofessional.com. When Micah is not engaged in professional activities, he enjoys spending time with his wife Jenny, daughters Madison and Ella, and son Carter.

6

"It Was The Right Thing To Do"

By Paul Taylor

Once in my thirty-year career I worked for a large brokerage firm. You know the kind. They have offices across the nation. They advertise constantly. They have become household names. Me, I had all the necessary licenses, both on the insurance side and the equities side.

A principal in the firm asked me to do something that was not right for the client. I resigned as quickly as I could get my office affairs in order. It was the right thing to do. I have never looked back.

I became an independent man with my own independent firm. I became a fiduciary.

I'm Paul Taylor. Today I run Capital Advisory Group, a boutique financial services firm in a beautiful part of North Carolina. Mooresville is our home base. It's on Lake Norman, stretching across several counties.

Many of our clients have recently relocated here. And why not? It is an easy commute to the headquarters of major firms. Cultural activities are abundant. There is room to move around in for those who enjoy the outdoors. Count me among those who can be found boating, golfing, or bird hunting in leisure hours.

Capital Advisory Group, with five employees, is small. Don't let that fool you. We have eight or nine investment professionals we call on for their particular expertise and also get support from a second-generation Michigan investment firm. We have an affiliation, too, with Morningstar, Inc. so their extensive database is available to us.

I get asked—often—about what is special about our firm. I'm proud to answer.

Our mission statement: "The Lord God is the center of our business. Through this belief we strive to make a difference in our clients' lives by doing more than financial planning." It's the foundation of my values and my passion for those I am blessed to serve.

Get to know me a little more by visiting our website, www.capitaladvisorygroup.net. It contains brief videos of me explaining who we are and how we can help. As stated, family is very important to me. The website will also share with you those closest to me—my wife and children. In one video I share a passion that my wife Rena and I share hosting clients for a boat ride or a meal at our house with me doing the cooking (It's a creative release for me).

At Capital Advisory Group we measure success not in bottom-line profits but in how we help people transition into retirement.

We are fiduciaries, who put the client's interest first, just as I did in my choice of employers. Only about 49 percent of people in our industry work as fiduciaries, according to a 2017 FINRA study. We don't answer to anybody except you. We have access to everything, not just a few products with some of them possibly overpriced. We're very boutique, because every client's needs are different. We take everyone's situation and look at it individually. We don't have a standard cure. Everyone needs to have a true financial plan that's going to meet their goals and objectives.

As a fiduciary, we work on a fee-based basis. Insurance products are sometimes the right answer for a client. Any time you work with an insurance company, built-in commissions are hard to avoid. However, we always seek to work in our clients' best interests, finding products that are the right fit for them. We're not persuaded to sell some insurance product based on the commissions the carriers pay us; putting your needs first is our priority.

At Capital Advisory Group, my staff of five is my back office. I'm the quarterback who pulled the team together.

The goal is to create a game plan. Someone comes in with all their records for an introductory session on the first appointment. We listen as they tell us their goals and what their challenge may be. We look at their investment history and run an analysis of the risk involved in their current holdings. We run a full background check on every single item in the portfolio. We will see what their income needs are and analyze, number one, the chances they might run out of money. Number two, based on their answers, we'll say whether they have more or less risk than we believe is prudent.

The following is a general description of services offered to illustrate how we serve clients, and not a discussion of specific product or security recommendations.

We vary our solutions to the client's circumstances and goals. There are some common concepts we apply. Consider, for example, a hypothetical couple of average means who are conservative and do not want to outlive their money.

We might suggest a three-bucket system. The first bucket would be for immediate income. This would be a one- to five-year bucket of short-term bonds or comparables for income over the next five years. We would then set up two other buckets. One would have more opportunity for growth. It would replenish anything we had placed in bucket one for income. Bucket three would be for extreme growth. It is designed not to be touched for at least ten years.

We consider where we are in the economic cycle before we craft a retirement plan for you. We want to make sure you have the proper mix in your portfolio. In today's low-interest environment, we might shy away from long-duration bonds. There may be another rate cut or two, but interest rates have to rise. The government is $22 trillion in debt and owners of government obligations will demand more interest on their money.

Everyone is different but many have similar concerns. Let's look at some of the questions or situations they present.

I'm often asked what we do if another 2008 comes along.

A cardinal rule is that we design a well-diversified account to begin with. I don't like for 100 percent of the assets to be in the stock market, ever. We will make changes in the portfolio when there is clear direction and there were clear directions in '08. So we are not averse to going to cash (money markets) and being patient. If a client is late in accepting that realization, we tell them they might as well stay in because the damage has been done and pulling out now would be the dumbest thing they could do.

Prospective clients want to know if we have an account minimum and the answer is easy: $250,000.

Financially sophisticated people, in particular, ask what products we use for the risky side of the portfolio. We might consider exchange traded funds (ETFs). They don't have the old-fashioned restrictive rules that mutual funds carry, number one. Number two, we might consider trading those ETFs virtually free through any of the major brokerages.

Some new clients arrive with portfolios that, frankly, are a mess. Perhaps they have bounced around the country from place to place as their career called for. They may have had several advisors over the years.

We do a portfolio analysis to show, hey this is where you are, here are the risks you have taken, your standard deviation (a measure of volatility) and the rate of return you have received.

Before we propose a solution, however, we identify any assets they are married to that have highly appreciated.

Many about-to-be retirees are concerned about what the economy may do in the first year or two of their retirement. What happens if it takes a nosedive?

It is true that if the market rises when you retire you're going to be fine and if the market turns down you may struggle for a long time.

An important part of that, however, is being realistic in what you withdraw each year.

You should never have 100 percent of your portfolio exposed to risk. You should have your portfolio protected in such a way that if the market is down, you can pull from the protected side.

There are clients who must make their funds last an exceptionally long time. Such as a husband with a considerably younger wife or a couple with a grown child with special needs.

A life insurance policy might be a great way to plan for that—if you can afford it. Your retirement plan needs to be built in a way that addresses, "Am I going to have enough money for the long retirement?" If not, we need to have this conversation anyway. You have to reduce your spending, go to plan b. How do you want to tackle that? A life insurance policy may still be the answer. If you don't

have enough money to pay the premium,
you work on reducing your spending to get
enough assets to pay the premium.

Some clients can be too frugal in retirement,
reluctant to dip into ample savings to splurge
just a little on themselves.

Financial freedom during retirement is oh so
nice. But so is financial freedom all through
life. When I can reach millennials directly
or through their parents or grandparents, I
preach: "Live below your means."

About The Author

Paul Taylor founded Capital Advisory Group twenty years ago. He is a fiduciary and was accepted as a member of the National Ethics Bureau in 2007. He is married with three children. There is another company with a similar name so look for him at www.capitaladvisorygroup.net. Or, phone him at 704-947-6985. His online video snippets give a feel for what his firm is like and strive to put you at ease the moment you walk in the door. Investment advisory and financial planning services offered through Advisory Alpha, LLC, a SEC Registered Investment Advisor. Insurance, consulting and education services offered through Capital Advisory Group. Advisory Alpha and Capital Advisory Group are not affiliated. The opinions expressed here are those of the author and do not necessarily represent those of Advisory Alpha, LLC

7

What Are Your Hopes, Dreams, And Goals?

By Robert Dorrestijn

Whenever a prospective client walks into my office, I ask them two questions:

"What are your hopes, goals, and dreams?"

"How much can you afford to lose?"

That opens the conversation and ultimately leads to two or three customized options for them to choose from in planning for retirement or making a course correction.

Me, I don't give financial advice. I act more as a guide. I show them the figures and ask, "Which do you prefer, Option A or Option

B?" Of course, by the time we've come up with a retirement plan, we've discussed their circumstances, life expectancy, spending and savings. They have shown me their financial records and usually have filled out a financial questionnaire.

On some occasions, they don't believe the numbers. I'm happy to push a ten-key calculator across the desk. "Here, run the numbers yourself." Some people can choose the best option only after doing the calculations themselves.

I bring a different background to constructing a retirement portfolio and a different attitude: It does not have to be complicated and my job is to uncomplicate it, to show a plan that meets their hopes, dreams and goals. Their job is to make the decision.

Some people look at the spelling of my last name—Dorrestijn—and guess what my lack of accent and spoken English have not revealed: I came to America with my family from The Netherlands at age twelve. Sure, English was a struggle for a few months. That was then, this is now.

Perhaps it is the running analogies that creep into my explanations or my trim body shape but many guess that I am an athlete. Actually, I'm a four-time qualifier for Iron Man triathlon world championships.

A sample analogy: "You've done a fine job of saving all your life. Now you're at the finish line. Why keep running? It is time to enjoy retirement and spend a little money."

I founded my company twenty years ago. Today our staff of six operates mainly out of offices in San Antonio, Austin and New Braunfels, Texas.

I don't have an armload of educational degrees and professional credentials. An insurance license, sure. I'm working on my securities license to reap the economies of skills. But mainly, the answer is: "I learned from twenty-four years of hard-earned insurance experience." I worked in the long-term care division of a major insurance company. Selling long-term care policies was easy once I mastered showing people that they pay for it out of their income from investments, not their monthly budget.

That carries over today at First Fidelity Tax and Insurance, LLC. Once we know your goals, once we know what kind of shape financially you are in, we can plot a course to the finish line.

The introductory process at First Fidelity is fairly standard but with some interesting twists. We meet some prospective clients through marketing seminars, some through referrals. We encourage all to attend a seminar, however, before coming in for the first interview. That way all have the same base of knowledge. That way, well, they aren't coming into a pizza shop expecting to order a deluxe hamburger.

At First Fidelity, annuities are what we do, mainly. Probably 80 percent of the time annuities are the product we use to guide clients to a retirement that meets their hopes, dreams and goals. The rest of the time the product of choice is certificates of deposit and life insurance.

In recent years we have been called upon to do considerable Social Security optimization. Taking Social Security at the right time can make a big difference in your life.

When clients walk in, we generally have them sit in the lobby for a few minutes. Relax, it may be the rest of your life we're talking about but take a moment to let the nervousness fade. Look around and see what is happening in a busy office. Chances are they may catch an advance glimpse of the whiteboard in my office. I always have one behind me. I meet with twelve or thirteen new people every week. Maybe it is the runner in me. Instead of sitting still, I like being active and taking notes. Sometimes the board is so full we cannot squeeze anything else in. You can be sure we start by writing on the board their hopes, their dreams and their goals.

The first visit is a time to assess the situation and give us some information we need to prepare a custom plan.

We're in no hurry to have the second visit, however. I want there to be some space, to give the client some time to think, to ask questions, to do research on our company. Perhaps read a good book by Patrick Kelly (*Is a Variable Annuity Right for Me?*, *The Retirement Miracle*, and *Stress-Free Retirement* are three).

A distance runner needs to learn how to pace herself. Don't start out too fast or you will pay for it later in the race. So it is with couples retiring. Don't try to accomplish everything at once. We put the things they want to do in some order of priority. What should be done in the first thirty days? In sixty days? In 180 days? At the end of thirty days we make sure that everything in the 30-day bucket was implemented. For some clients, it is getting a will. In the next ninety days it might be that we want to move some money.

Retirement is a long-distance run. Prioritize things and do them in stages.

"How much can you afford to lose?" If the client's answer is "zero," we steer them away from the stock market. If they bring $1 million into retirement and $600,000 will meet their needs that may go into annuities while the ancillary money into other investments.

Annuities have a wonderful reputation, the guy on TV running them down while touting other products, notwithstanding. Annuities need to be used in the right manner, however. You don't want to use an annuity in a tax-sheltered account. There is no benefit to having something double tax sheltered.

Modern annuities can provide a steady, guaranteed stream of income with riders that provide some inflation protection.

Let's look at a few questions we get and how sometimes annuities are the solution.

I've stashed a considerable amount in my 401(k). Am I OK?

We get asked that by Baby Boomers all the time. The answer is how much is in your emergency fund and may circumstances force you to retire before you are 59 and one-half. You don't want a huge tax bill when you take the money out plus a 10 percent penalty. Divert some future savings into your emergency fund if necessary.

Should we sell our second home?

Probably no. Personally, I'm a big believer in real estate and it keeps going up. I generally match the client with a solid real estate broker. Holding onto the house or renting it out often is the better option. Avoiding a taxable event is one reason. Leaving the house as an inheritance may not. (We have a tax attorney on retainer who meets with our clients in our office.) Another reason is that renting out a house may bring a rate of return of 10 percent on your cost basis. Where are you going to get that kind of return?

One client wanted to downsize by selling his house and moving into a smaller one. The way it was going to pencil out, he discovered, was that he would be paying double the amount of money for half the square footage.

A lady had an ancillary amount of $90,000 in the stock market. She wanted to retire by Christmas and use that portion of her money to take $5,000 or $6,000 out each year and travel.

I asked how much she could afford to lose and she said none. We quickly pulled her out of the market.

I have a grown child with special needs. How can I see that he has a secure future after I am gone?

That's one reason we have attorneys on retainer. San Antonio has a larger military presence than many cities. Unfortunately, we've run into a lot of veterans who dealt with Agent Orange and therefore have children with some medical issues. Our attorney has set up quite a few special needs trusts.

My wife is twenty years younger than I am. How can I provide for her longer life expectancy?

One way where we have had success is to use the income from an annuity to buy life insurance. The life insurance feeds the special needs trust. That's a very clean way to do it. The client may choose a fixed index annuity with an income rider that guarantees an income and a universal life insurance policy that is a guaranteed way out.

My spouse isn't very savvy about financial matters. I make all the financial decisions. Must he come in with me?

We prefer it. I absolutely demand that I talk to the husband or wife at least on the phone unless I am told it is segregated, not joint money.

Sometimes the spouse is present and says, "I don't understand."

Then you either sit down and explain it using different terminology or you schedule another session.

It is our job to educate people. The amount of money they bring to retirement results in probably the largest financial decisions of their life. If the financial terminology is confusing to someone who is a pre-retiree but a newcomer to the financial world, it is our job to make it less complicated. One reason I wanted to contribute to this book is to explain in my own words, not just orally, but in a different way. In a way they can read and read again and ask me questions when we visit again.

I am my husband's second wife and the kids wanted to make sure the house, which he bought before we were married, goes to them. That is in the will.

"Whoa! Where are you going to live after his demise?" We called on our attorney who drafted up a trust for the husband and his house. Upon his death, the wife can continue to live in it. She is responsible for maintenance, taxes and everything else. She is not allowed to sell it or rent it out. If she vacates the house under her free will, then it goes to the kids.

It isn't all work, no play at our company. We host four social events a year with just one self-imposed rule: There is absolutely no discussion of business. It is a chance for people of retirement age to get out of the house and socialize. We have a movie date for our clients who live in south Texas. Country music is big here so in another event we hire a band, go to one of the local dance halls and let them rip. Everyone, including us, has fun.

Retirement is a transition. With proper financial planning, we have the time, the freedom and the means to do what we want to do. Like a triathlete, our pace slows down in the later stages. With determination, however, we can still do what we enjoy doing.

I ran a race in Indonesia one time and I met an eighty-two-year-old and an eighty-five-year-old who were doing the race. With proper training, proper nutrition and proper rest, it is amazing what the body can accomplish. We were at the award ceremony but the guys were still running. The race was over, right? The organizers had shut down the support team, the clean-up crew already was busy. The guys were out there just plugging along. They were going to finish the race.

Whether cruising on a running course, a cruise ship, a golf course, or at a bridge tournament, that can be you.

At First Fidelity we would like to help.

About The Author

Robert Dorrestijn is president of First Fidelity Tax and Insurance in Austin, San Antonio, and New Braunfels, Texas.

8

The Case For Equities In Every Portfolio

By Stuart Dickson

Equities, I believe, are the single greatest wealth creator in the last one hundred years. There are plenty of evidence-based science and academic studies to support that statement. I believe every portfolio should start with a base of some type of equity.

There are three traps to avoid in building these portfolios. Actually, one of the biggest obstacles to overcome is the individual's risk tolerance or fear of taking risk. Today's generation of retirees had parents or grandparents who went through the Great Depression. Often those memories and attitudes have been passed down.

Then too, sharp market corrections sometimes happen, like the Great Recession of '08 and '09. Human nature is quick to panic and sell—precisely at the wrong moment.

Today's retirees must finance twenty-five to thirty-five years living off of Social Security, a pension (if they are lucky), and their investments. If retirees do nothing to get aboard the train of the greatest wealth creator in order to have market gains bolster their portfolio, they risk seeing inflation and unpredictable medical expenses decimate their life savings and their lifestyle over time.

For investment advisors, our challenge is to construct portfolios that are diversified, with layers on both the safe and risk sides, and with a safety buffer and an exit strategy driven by prudence, not panic, in times of distress. Properly done, the market growth can protect and bolster their current degree of financial independence. We are tasked with educating clients so they can understand and be comfortable in making the necessary financial decisions.

I'm Stuart Dickson, co-CEO at Vimvest Advisors in Sarasota, Florida. We're a family firm with mother, Margaret Hixon, the founder and president, and brother Phillip Dickson, a co-CEO as well. We are well represented in this book with Margaret Hixon and financial advisor Bradley Johnson contributing their own chapters.

I'm on the equities side although I am licensed to do insurance as well. I am a fiduciary and operate on a fee-only basis.

Financial planning is in my blood. My mother, who has been in the industry for thirty-one years, would talk about it at the dinner table with her husband. Like a child in a multilingual household, picking up the second language of "finance" came effortlessly to me. It clicked further when I was in college reading about finances, investments and taxes.

I remember attending a class one day on taxation by a professor who had never actually put together a financial plan and probably had never looked at one. His approach was to minimize taxes in the early years but not account for taxes that would inevitably arise later in retirement. He wanted to fully fund 401(k)s and IRAs.

My strategy was much different but had a wildly different outcome if I ran with the correct software. When I showed this to my professor, he asked me to never do that again in front of the class.

I'm a fiduciary and proud of it. That means putting the client's interests first, before the company's or mine. There was a movement to require all advisors and salespeople to be fiduciaries, but unfortunately it was not implemented. Operating as a fiduciary removes the temptation to sell the client a product that pays the highest commission. That is not in the client's *best* interest.

Unfortunately, the word "fiduciary" has been thrown around far too much. In shopping for a financial advisor, see if you can answer these five questions. If you can't, you probably are not working with a fiduciary. The questions are:

1. What are the internal/external fees and the percentage of the investment?

2. What is that in dollars? Now, if you don't know those two things up front, you're probably not working with a fiduciary.

3. How did the investment perform in 2008 and 2009? So what was the risk? Those

years were the most recent downturn we've seen and it was pretty catastrophic to a few people. If the investment you are in can drop 30 percent, did you know that?

4. What is the tax liability? Are there any kind of tax savings, any way to collect the income tax-free? Is there a way to harvest losses at the end of the year? If you earn a rate of return of 20 percent, what tax rate are you going to pay? Any annuity is going to pay out money taxed as ordinary income. In a brokerage account and held over a year, that same 20 percent could be taken out at a lower tax rate as long-term capital gains.

5. What is the liquidity of the investment? Are you going to be penalized if you need to get your money out before the term ends, as in a certificate of deposit, annuity or other variable contract?

That's a good base to use in looking for a financial advisor. If you don't know the answers, I highly doubt you're working with a fiduciary.

So what is my approach to the market? Let's start with building a portfolio.

There are three things that a portfolio cannot do:

You cannot pick individual stocks. Markets are random and unpredictable and having individual stock selections nowadays represents too much risk.

You cannot "time" the market. You cannot come in and out of the market. Time *in* the market is more important than timing the market.

You cannot "track record" invest. You cannot look at how well someone has done over the last five or ten years. If you pull your 401(k) money out to a self-directed IRA and invest with that person, guess what? During the next three or four years they will likely underperform the market, perhaps by 30 or 40 percent. So, you need to use asset allocation and weigh the assets depending on your risk tolerance.

Under this approach, the goal for the equity portion of the portfolio is to match a given index. But remember, we are diversified and have invested in other types of products. The return of the *entire* portfolio will be different, probably less in the long run than a stock index.

Most investors want the returns of the S&P 500 index. But they can't swing with, can't stomach the up-and-down risk of the S&P. You may know that it was down 50 percent in 2008 and 2009.

Can we harvest good gains and reduce the volatility through asset allocation? Yes, I believe we can.

Our clients will have a healthy mix of what they can afford of equity versus fixed income. The income side isn't just any type of fixed income. It's going to be all high quality, short-term fixed income—nothing over five years. The duration will probably average about 1.9 years because interest rates are at all-time lows. And we can look back at the history of the market and see that almost 9.9 out of 10 times, stocks will beat fixed income over every rolling ten years.

We can use proven results and academic studies to build our clients' portfolios from three premiums that are available. First, we know equities will beat fixed income. Second, we know there is a large and small company premium. In the long run, small companies will return more than large companies. (Of course, the risk is greater but remember we are not investing in individual stocks.) And third, if we invest in value companies as a sector—dividend payers that seem to be underpriced—we'll collect a premium in the form of dividends while we wait.

We're not trying to chase the hot trend of the day, or the new ETFs (exchange-traded funds, the modern evolution of mutual funds), or the new stock allocation of the day. We're looking for portfolios that can last twenty years, not twenty weeks or twenty months.

Let's return to the S&P's 50 percent drop in '08/'09. It is a lesson in educating the client to not panic, and to look at a well-constructed portfolio and how it performs over the long run. We believe in true diversification by not having all of your money on, say, just the risk side or the safe side.

If another 2008 were to happen, would you be able to afford your lifestyle? What are your "I need" and "I want" numbers? If the markets are down 30 to 40 percent but 100 percent of your money is in the market, no portfolio could weather that. You need to have some money on the safe side. And "safe side" to us means that no matter what happens in the marketplace, you cannot lose a dime on that portion of the portfolio.

We had clients who retired in 2008 and 2009 and their experience shows the rewards of not panicking. Only a couple clients wanted to cash out because they got scared and another advisor had sat them down. Basically, they came to us and wanted to be all cash. We talked them out of it and they did extraordinarily well.

They weathered those two "down" years and their portfolios rebounded. They and our other clients in diversified portfolios were in the green before 2010 ended. And from 2010 on they have been in the green and participating in this equity bull run that we've seen.

These diversified clients did not lose a dollar of their money on the safe side. So when the market dropped and maybe a portion of their portfolio went down 20 or 30 percent, they no longer needed to go to that "well." And they allowed that well to replenish while they went to another well.

Stocks are a great wealth generator. Yet, we'll put some safe side products in the portfolio even though they do not return as much over the long run. The downturns are why.

Let's look at a safe product, a fixed index annuity.

A fixed index annuity is a formulated investment, and absolutely the insurance company gets paid because what they're giving you is probably a five or ten-year contract. What's the liquidity of the investment? If you're going to give your money to an insurance carrier for ten years, you must understand that commitment and loss of liquidity.

So there can be fees and (opportunity) costs. These are income products that are going to generate some type of guaranteed income down the road. There is a free product out there we use that does not cost the investor anything. If you put $100,000 in and at the end of the first year the market did nothing, you would still have $100,000. So, there is no internal cost.

Now say the market goes up 10 percent the second year and the investor only received 4 percent or 5 percent. The opportunity costs there could be perceived as 6 percent or 5 percent. I absolutely would not call that a fee. That's an opportunity cost.

It's vital to understand the caps, spreads and participation rates because if you're not working with a fiduciary, those are the other questions you need to go through to really understand your contract. I suspect that nine out of ten advisors don't fully understand the underwritten contracts.

But let's say in the third year of the annuity contract, the market drops 20 percent. Now, the first year we got a zero. The second year we got 4 percent and the third year the market drops 20 percent and we get a big fat zero.

I don't know what type of "fee" you would call that, but it would be peace of mind knowing that your account did not drop 20 percent. You are never going to get all of the market return, but you certainly will not get any of the market downturns in a fixed index annuity if sold properly.

Finally, I would say that the majority of our clients have portfolios of $500,000 or more. We do put on dinner seminars and, well, some who attend may be more interested in the dinner than the seminar. That's fine. We allow those prospective clients to sit next to clients who've been with us five and ten years, who show up because they genuinely want the education.

So they sit together and talk. Could you imagine any other financial planner doing that?

The newcomers are getting feedback from our long-term clients on how the system works. Basically, they're asking, "Do you like the people? Do you trust them? Do you think they can do the job?"

And our clients sell it for us.

About The Author

Stuart Dickson is co-CEO of Vimvest Advisors.

Appendix

About The Editors

Mark Gaffney is the founder of Mark Edward Gaffney, a boutique consulting and marketing firm for the financial services industry. His Elite Advisor Client List reads like a "Who's Who" of the financial services industry. Since 2002, he has coached, consulted, and trained hundreds of financial professionals across the United States. His "Image and Brand" advertising agency approach to financial marketing has made him a prominent authority throughout the national advisor community.

In his more-than-twenty-five-year marketing career, Gaffney's list of credits include: renowned national marketing strategist, executive producer of numerous television shows and radio programs across the United

States, keynote speaker, and the best-selling coauthor of *The Winning Way*.

Gaffney has worked with multi-billion-dollar corporations as well as start-ups and business entrepreneurs at all phases of development. His marketing strategies have returned hundreds of millions in production for his financial clients. Gaffney lives in Tampa, Florida with his wife Jennifer and their four children Isabella, Alexandrea, Liam, and Luke.

Henry DeVries writes a weekly column for Forbes.com, is the coauthor of the McGraw-Hill international best-selling book *How To Close A Deal Like Warren Buffett*, and is the former vice president of the international financial services firm Foresters. Today he is CEO of Indie Books International.

Don Sevrens was a career journalist and editor with a metropolitan daily newspaper, the *San Diego Union-Tribune*, who now edits and writes financial books.